Free Verse Editions

Edited by Jon Thompson

The North Face of Juliau, Six

Overyellow

The Poem as Installation Art

Nicolas Pesquès

Translated by Cole Swensen

Parlor Press
Anderson, South Carolina
www.parlorpress.com

Parlor Press LLC, Anderson, South Carolina, 29621

Library of Congress Cataloging-in-Publication Data on File

Names: Pesquáes, Nicolas, author. | Swensen, Cole, 1955-
translator.
Title: Overyellow : the poem as installation art / Nicolas Pesques
;   translated by Cole Swensen.
Other titles: Surjaune, installation. English
Description: Anderson, South Carolina : Parlor Press, [2017] |
Series: Free verse editions | Series: The north face of Juliau ; six
Identifiers: LCCN 2017038918 | ISBN 9781602358973 (pbk. :
alk. paper)
Classification: LCC PQ2676.E7829 S8713 2017 | DDC
841/.914--dc23
LC record available at https://lccn.loc.gov/2017038918

1 2 3 4 5

Cover design by Erica Mena and Cole Swensen.
Printed on acid-free paper.

Parlor Press, LLC is an independent publisher of scholarly and
trade titles in print and multimedia formats. This book is available
in paperback and ebook formats from Parlor Press on the World
Wide Web at http://www.parlorpress.com or through online and
brick-and-mortar bookstores. For submission information or to
find out about Parlor Press publications, write to Parlor Press,
3015 Brackenberry Drive, Anderson, South Carolina, 29621, or
email editor@parlorpress.com.

Contents

Preface

Nicolas Pesquès has been working on a single project for over twenty years: *La face nord de Juliau* (*The North Face of Mount Juliau*); it's now twelve volumes long. On the one hand, it's a work about place—about the attempt to construct, through writing, the possibility of place in the external world. It's an attempt based on the recognition that the "external world," too, is constructed of and through language, and so Pesquès's interrogation of the mountain that dominates his landscape becomes an interrogation of language, of how it brings us the world and how it simultaneously denies us access to it. But on the other hand, the series is also—one could even say, is only—about color, about the irrepressibility and the impact of the vivid. Slowly growing throughout the collection is a suggestion that color is alive in a way that nothing else is. And that color alone has the power to exhaust language, to mitigate its tyranny over our lives. In this, volume six, the color is yellow—the vivid yellow of the English broom that blooms outrageously, uproariously, all over the mountainside every year in June. Pesquès here views that yellow as a work of installation art consisting of the word YELLOW constructed of enormous letters and erected on the side of the hill. It becomes a physical shout that fills the visual, audio, and cognitive fields with an endlessly opening, infinitely detailed color. And language becomes a way, finally, simply to be able to look at it, to witness it. And that witness becomes in turn a way to participate in it, to fuse for a split-second with its brilliant, blinding life.

Overyellow

What color do we live in after the eyes?
and when does it begin?

YELLOW opens a space for reading, and we're attached to it
seed, hill, painting compressed

and able to fit into new sentences

. . .

when yellow is compressed like this, YELLOW becomes something said
several verbs, several feelings

owed to something else it resembles, as if one more letter
had been added to the alphabet

yellow seen and YELLOW read.

Once YELLOW is said, the poem becomes unthinkably real.
You see that you no longer know what you see. You see that what
you wanted in the forest of English broom cannot be taken in.

A cyst as injurious as it is magnificent.

An extract, a lack of resemblance incorporated.

It's not that I've given up the hill, nor encountered a miracle
of language.
It's just that what remains impossible is nonetheless very present;
the pain seems to stretch all the way to the expressible.

Undescribed, indescribable.
YELLOW somehow digitized, and blindingly fine.

. . .

yellow hindered by its splendor.

The color of love will be thwarted.
These days, it amounts to a collapse into certitude.

YELLOW on a tomb
my body from somewhere else, my other bodies.

. . .

making the landscape into its own inverse:
tender animals, constrained trees,
black wind.

Overthrown, double-exposure—and at the same time, supportive.
To believe that it's enough. That breathing is abolished, that the echo
of the heels is binding

Yellow not denied and NOT-YELLOW accepted.
A convergence of circumstances. A vital minimum.

. . .

A minimum of silence.

decapitated law,
so poor, so little an image.

. . .

YELLOW-LAW right up against the eyes, air's awls, raising the hill,
the watching body

a single sentence could, through infirmity, find its duration and
assuage the pain.

Out there in the landscape, it's the YELLOW that's added,
both trimming
and giving breath, a margin in which the broom maneuvers.

It's lit up, like turbulence
letting what's already lost through words and pictures
go back and settle on the horizon.

. . .

YELLOW is the impetus. Impetus is the evidence that the eye needs,
a lighthouse emitting night.

We think that, faced with a landscape, words can
construct a reproduction, but it's something else
entirely, and the result is oddly
so hard to live with, so much less Edenic
than its model.

. . .

I wish the sentence could be seen coming out of the wall,
carrying off its chasm, reading the woods.

Perhaps on a tree trunk, at least a finger for each line, I could write like never before.

In horizontal bands, yellow's meaning, the pictured force.

. . .

Intermittent pink at each step through the undergrowth.
The violence of the repeated days accrues as a watermark.

But it's engraved on the INSIDE.

. . .

Because of the body, because it's avid to multiply the incompatible languages all around it.
Which is why it can be neither inside nor elsewhere.

Other tomb, other resemblance.

My example will have been the following: as I crossed the forest of broom, I was both stopped and started. What halted me could be described to infinity, which is to say superstitious, painful, comparable to YELLOW in terms of strangulation.

For inhaling.

. . .

The opposite of *because*: as if enormous night had been demolished exposing the wells, the stone walls in dust.

The time of a sentence. The true workings of stone.

This project is based in the hope that the forest of broom will
happen again.

This object condenses and runs it.
It enlarges the circle, the mirror of the estate. It spreads the brain.

Like, at the end of the road, a wall of air.

. . .

YELLOW ambient and resistant. Brake poem. Hoisted-plunged.
A garden grown sudden.

Gathered to the woods, to the gestures: curves and graphics appear.
They over-invent the landscape.

The fact that forgetting is the only experience that's real means that
the coordinates scaffold the beating heart of the image. What I can
touch. Then they abandon me too.

. . .

I consider the description of immediacy, of the variety of particles.

Hill fully arranged. Sentence in a state of shock.
The frontispiece of the ruin.

A singularity, a mountain LEGIBLE by squaring and unlinking.

Hill nailed like a thistle to the door, a rat under the moon.
A sculpture.

. . .

YELLOW ready to revoke the permission to stop seeing.
The already gone-dark, the already slipped from memory.

Then the fall, the chest on fire. The lead everywhere organizing it all.

The sentence extends the arm. The experiment will always be outside. But how can you inject anything into something that has neither strict boundaries nor intimacy?

Autonomous, robotic, adventurous, YELLOW connects us physically, purely concretely.

. . .

Just looks like an implant of the outside. YELLOW gatherer and its book.

Its madonna slopes.
Succeeding better with its metal, without the story being visible.

Explosion of the gentle by-passer, all in letters.
Industrial poem following through on its contraction.

Commutative hill, placed on its platform, like a dry garden struck
motionless by music.

. . .

Lacquered, which is to say written like a background.
YELLOW of the living ridges.

Barring the hillside—grass and concrete, grass and neon—ruptured
by objective color.

Organic YELLOW, just as the broom.
Each step like crystal stepping.

Moved without comment, self-lit by poem, and poem, like a
difference you could sleep with.

. . .

With a non-linear, unground, sweet-sharp precision.
The eyes like all rejection gone. The grass now obvious.
But how to get there?

I see a use-value in this YELLOW, as if, at a turn in the path, you stumbled upon a block of stone or steel placed there. Justified in some unknown way. Surprise without a face.

A mass. A sculpted capital letter. A pointer.
Heavy and deeply discrete.

YELLOW bollard. Finally identical word embedded in the landscape. Integrated thing.

To run up against without stopping.
To walk as if reading. To write and vice-versa.

A precise and well-tended life.

YELLOW thanks to a pattern that doesn't circumvent it. Non-foreign body.
Real body rooted in distinction.

A solid moment, lost, extremely clear.

Not restored. A new kiss on the mouth.
The same but correlated, transsexualized by the forest of broom.

Opened like an order. Destroyed like a passage.

A new exaltation. A fertile winch.

YELLOW son of the body and the term. A statue without ancestors.

Slow desire, not promised; it can only be expressed as the evolution of stone.

A form against which writing extinguishes itself.

Meticulous absorption of what might seem indivisible.
Painted mountain, written slope. Everyone raking over
the setting-on-fire.

Flowers at the ends of branches are born in a rush.

The mountain's skin and my leaping eye.
And that yellow over there, projecting, such as it is in its shivering.

. . .

First-born landscape, like they call the poem a non-poem.
Or the pain of precise YELLOW.

. . .

Visuality that requires a specific body. A reading that presents the
broom fused to its construction.
A grouped group.

The wall of beautiful perspective, become theater of my hill,
in the sense that you could do without a mirror.
The beautiful wall holding on to torment.

. . .

An entity composed of colored fields.
There's something of painting in that, or of grass, or of shadow.
Nothing but self-sacrifice and technique.

. . .

Another way of writing, of moving the woods, of depicting the
yellow turned to hill.

Religious reflexes disappear. Only the body caught short
invents its response.
I continue to describe. I do nothing else.

That's the visible part. You can open it, let something incarnated in,
something touching.
To maintain its decency, its erotic surface.
Its reach joined to its disappearance.

. . .

Something as strong as an object in a niche,
more alarming than a fetish.
YELLOW causes a coupling.
YELLOW bowls me over as much as the crossing, as much as its
falling into color.

Overyellow, The Installation Piece

One step, then another, sculpted
a priori, a providence

have we tuned our eyes as what sharpens bursts forth

are we in this light?

. . .

it's put in place, it's appeared like a monument
like a better presence

the surface is calm, positioned; it breathes in

the object surpasses itself, verbs will come
the object achieves them

a form leaning on its echoes
conceived to produce, to sensitize

but above all, it's written and nature takes it
nature is furnished

. . .

a principle of intervention, a lawless landscape
I'm approaching the same programmatic zone
as Paul Cezanne

to not fall from the sky, to not seem natural
an air of immersion and of things never there

an object from then on, poem like that with landscape

. . .

landscape around an announcement

. . .

a text-effect in the field
a hill read at the same time as a hill

one step and then another, dug out loud
once inscribed, the background moves

for once, the disappearance is truly solid
we're inside, and the day is enough.

this impeccable word is everything but a word
something found mid-trail that doesn't tremble

. . .

strange to come back to you with this permanence,
in this theater
up to the shoulders in night

the frozen disorder, welcoming

a smile of shadow, another of shine

the whole body invited, as well as this assonance

a work has started and now it pulls back
or rather we owe it this indivisibility

sculpture like birth, alphabet

nature made for that, neither attentive nor warm
simply made for it. Perfect.

. . .

a work inhabited by the outside
inhabited which is to say disconcerted, humbling
till jaws clenched, wholly facing everything

loving by writing

object recaptured, escaped-recaptured

chest on the prowl, capable of putting together

something real

. . .

we arrive from every direction
trails that are frames

but it remains imprinted, transported by expression

. . .

from another angle, the body hardens, it's amazed
the poem reigns, solitude is vanquished

to write in statue
to feel carried off, suffocated by a beginning
by the sense of color, the construction of the impulse

for speed and great height

. . .

we're living, we're inside the image
because it's written outside
working against that which no longer transports you

and so we fall with the formula,
with the icon
and loving so suddenly is frightening

the letters are ten feet high
and appropriately deep and wide

which means that OVERYELLOW stretches some 30 yards
through the landscape
though the scale can be changed to fit the site

we must be more precise, decide on the exact shade, write it out,
make drafts, sketches, follies

building castles on the spot

. . .

the rules of installation invent their own cave walls,
their painted bison
OVERYELLOW is the name of the god of labor and the lively

a reclining body that watches us, its breasts seized by diction
making the hill come forward

the letters have the same solidity as the oaks behind them
nailed to the heart of their precision

proposition lashed down and grafted onto nature
which created it in the same color

. . .

sweeping off the contemporary, implanting the contemporary

a stretch of OVERYELLOW wall
the return of the hill to culture

. . .

in fact, I construct a piece of color
and the whole outside world becomes legible

a generative megalith

you see the bars that hold the piece up, you see how they're attached
which creates an outside;
the cover begins, the book sinks in

. . .

a corner of paradise that we'll call an entrance

a monument full of its opening

. . .

the pain could fade, sparkling in its own way
its so-transported way

so drunk and surfaced, like a sentence on the table
a celestial scaffolding

one step then another in the open air
a theater and its armature, something hurled

returning to the future
and yet when you face it you are anchored
engulfed in the face of the field

. . .

of a thing seen, of a seeing attached to the said

you know the world
and you no longer know anyone

we watch desire unfurling in a single voice.

and not a word after a single one.

. . .

poem installed, taken as a piece

. . .

it's not even as yellow as all that
the project is not to know the color
nor to exhaustively describe it

it is rather to grow

one step, then a stamp
in a single plane of depth
the hill unleashes its augmentation

a double without a shadow:
foliage, grass, the elements of a body

a film in and of life
the failure of one difference between and between

the failure to distinguish the time
of an invention from what preceded it

. . .

access is possible, it's that turned inside-out

inside is a direction under the sky, a step toward
and yet not stopping the entrance

yellow stripped of all precondition
OVERYELLOW that extends its accession
landscape all in one, permanently positioned, book included

the project: construct something
that keeps yellow from stopping

the work constructs the conditions that would make the work possible

an acquired unpredictability, the appearance of wealth
an excess that is strictly, thoroughly hill

marvel upon marvel

. . .

one step, and then the one in front
the installation of OVERYELLOW at the same time as itself

a piece that's being written while it's already there
as if you could be cut off from everything and at the same time born

yellow and crossing

writing would have happened, would have been this cradle
beneath any climate whatsoever

OVERYELLOW or nature entirely preserved

. . .

an animality slipped between the interstices
of the future

outside, being intimacy, became so suddenly

nature head-on as if from the other side
a gift of gentleness, a radical gift

of great clarity, legible before everything and yet still a hurdle

neither lack nor hope to the finished piece, consumed
nor disarmament

it has memorized the smile of every natural death
it has compressed parental power
seizing the divisible with a single hand

. . .

even now that I know, now that the color has been stopped
I still couldn't do it again nor make the leap

. . .

a very slow silhouette tells yellow the time, the season

you can stay inside, you're always out

reading is the same as completing a step: a concept
then a sexuality

passersby enjoy its profile, the back of it
from all perspectives; it becomes an emotional object

a title

the whole thing holds together
you see the irregular bars that connect its parts

it leans on something or is free, like a wreck in good shape
there's always a possibility that the poem will become real
that there will be nothing left inside

the complete opposite of the inner experience
to be an object or nothing, no longer self

its self turned inside-out, in sync with the woods

it's not understanding that makes the text accessible
it's the return
the fact that the artifice is positioned exactly where the natural is
waiting for the same lighting

OVERYELLOW or a shack for a fox
fauve neon, integrated object

. . .

reflect, write, post
sky mixed with the edge of the grass

the blackbird in the almond trees in March

. . .

a body that writes, that comes out of the shadow
finds dust again

an object tore from me the name of its desire
and the name of its effect

a scent of text, the caprice of a whirlwind

a desire that grows with its realization

. . .

both the black of all colors and the opposite of a tomb

a sort of dry enchantment, gnawing,
greeting appearance

and now at hand there is a story, the visual
aggravation of yellow

. . .

perhaps independence is simply a matter of phrasing
and is the basis of everything we do

Overyellow: The Dissolution

1

Then it will be forgotten as if forgotten by its shock
language never found again

one more step and then the lock
the tumult

. . .

the hill once again resembles the contents of its appearance:
the greater speed of capacity and ruins

because appearance is nothing more, an exact separation
that leaves the erasure of appearance entire and alone

the written hill

seeing only the ravaging
of beauty without a future

. . .

place includes its own erasure, an added visibility

looking refuses all antecedent, reading as well
there's no other solution, none at all

a little more YELLOW each time history rights the balance

it never would have worked without an amplified jungle
and a separation

. . .

what's the meaning of a excised flux that yet remains?

an inassimilable object beyond the flowering cherries

. . .

the poem could have appeared on any surface
now it welcomes the place, constitutes a process
the perspective of a change of perspective

and at the same time it's precise,
it's written to make a single thing look different all over

the instructions have been destroyed
and with them the reference to a new world

the tear

. . .

sensing the limit within a disinterested vertigo
as in any language or hillside

any cut or collapse

the very reason for all presence

beauty thus brandished is indelible

which is what is different about the animal
although, as it's being wrenched out, the quarry of writing
keeps the flesh open

logic under the absolute rule of its teeth
the body in a state of demand

. . .

writing would then be able to account
beyond the cut,
for that from which the writer is split
without experiencing it as death

as so the calm is broken
beneath the magnetism of the landscape

. . .

as if writing could synchronize a world
with its own detachment

a world magestically bribed
in the face of its lack of sovereignty

you wouldn't think language could reduce the distance
created by its own apparition

with OVERYELLOW you see the landscape from the back
enriched by a gap

. . .

I take notes
as if it were a project

I confirm a dry silence and refuse glossolalia

. . .

OVERYELLOW is not another English broom
it's a magnifying glass polished in the direction of distraction
and synthesis

a neologism of nature

how can it be blended?

the hillside is already perfect, it's already lost
the simplifying intensity of a color mixes only with weakness

just as the living dissipate

what remains is a concretion, an agglutinated forgotten

. . .

naming is an extension that splits the world in two
each phrase plants a kiss on each side, a caesura opening
the distance
which ruins it but causes feeling;
it makes whatever it touches come into being

appearing so solid
OVERYELLOW builds the sun

It projects language by making it stand
life circulates

. . .

and suddenly we're in the same world

passing from one to the same in full color
without blending them

. . .

once more abandoned to the measure of a chasm
impeccably designed by a form beyond proposition

the separation dates further back than *logos*
the myth already gathers the steps of nature, makes
them intelligible

a new way of being for things
the same smell

broom will not be denied by its color
but articulated, increased
as if nature was there, waiting within nature

in its excessive manner, oozing

yellow, above all, non-cerebral

things were never destined to become speech
but once speech is established, things endlessly flee

their insubordination is positive, their colors ejaculatory

OVERYELLOW introduces a walled light, the latch of night

. . .

a paean to the dense and the tight

with no feeling but the disinterred
an harassment that would have found its stone

and its stone's juice

II

OVERYELLOW erected and minted half-way up the slope
as intimately nailed as Emily on her bed of breaks

a metronome solo

. . .

inaudible before

beheaded by speech
which looks back at its body   without memory

yellow rejected to let silence cease and reign

the eyes are best at making the crossing

then the tongue, cutting through the living

then an installation became possible close to the nerve
and the English broom we live among

the construction only resists after an enjambment
that's also found in nature

I gave form to a piece of the past
that strikes the eyes

a reservoir of causality
a moment not dismembered   but frozen

that is now its own dissection

. . .

an obstruction removed by the speed of reading
a rhythm that constitutes a landscape

yellow to the ends of its nerves
linking story to story until they're destroyed

we enter into shadow, and it's the same labyrinth
the same exchange of endstop and divination

the end of the eye and the recoil of the murmur

. . .

a way of counter-pointing
the suppression of carriers, the word music itself
faints

as yellow as the night of time, such total love

a condensation at the heart of language
resembling a natural phenomenon
broadcasting a clearing

yellow not cooled down, not liquid
a special state of expression

. . .

to make it definite: this would be OVERYELLOW
instantly dissolved: a story

OVER as in overprinting,
it is material, yes, but even more,
hardened by accretion,

as if I had inhaled a star
captured its dust

.   .   .

crushed by the capacity of the instant to go through all that

everything mixed together,
going through this brown

riveted to the here, riveted to the eyes,
nailed to a democratic meadow

to the heart-yellow of a knee

so strident
the liquid hand   in the woods

blocking the threshold, introducing yellow

my measured life, my better eyes
my coffin of life

. . .

to touch what names the past, what pushes the horizon back

that the image might become something rawer than raw
a jaw

around which one falls in turning

here's exactly where OVERYELLOW spreads out
that which is side-lined, drawing from future powers

impeccably colored body emptied of its honey

. . .

a work similar to that of separation

visibility in a single time by the touch of a new-born name
as physical as any emanation

a dirigible on the inside of pleasure

an object in the world
the meeting of several bodies

a drought which does some good
as does color, filling in surfaces
filling in angles

. . .

to have disappeared once stamped by the stated

in the work there was first the field
the forest of English broom, the gate of the moment

to have disappeared or to open your eyes again

III

In the beginning there was nothing but immediacy

a continual source of forgetting
that doesn't need us

. . .

later sensation proceeded from abstraction
while a word cut-out occupied the slope

from one to the other, it looks like slight-of-hand
whose expression would keep a secret
though the secret is not its own

in the end, a sacrificial yellow strikes my eyes
the body won

verbs don't allow continual rupture
they can't survive the immediate

yellow goes up to a billion and then crashes

the collection could be called consequence
but it's an invention, an unexpected eyelid

a polished providence on the back of a color

we'll never get done with it

and yet it's nothing but incarnation
an aggregate of reflexes, of resemblances, you could call it a hillside

on the face of which yellow brakes and fuses

. . .

fluidity and geometry on a single side
one field of impulse at a time

we'll be no longer intertwined

would have put something unified there
the evidence of subtraction

yellow often constitutes the verb to be
based on what it's leaving, maintaining itself

around which YELLOW conjugates what we no longer see
this always-there of a hillside

once eclipsed, the object deifies what it reveals
erases its multiples
piles of bodies full of knotted reactions

that which is said now exists

. . .

the altar of the word remains out in the open
black magic of those who do not come:

the undergrounds, the biographical
those who don't know what's flowing inside the flow

those who can't be indistinct, can't be simultaneous
coming to shore inside of the overflow
over the continual disappearance of the underground tangle

or maybe this, or maybe that
in a single field

a trembling from the plinth

this yellow that would speak
this crushing the whole body into the exit of language

. . .

if that took hold
if the imperious color crossed over

why does this necessity take us apart?

seeing it again would mean a new place to live

a lovely day, the years to come, the traces of bright pink
how many times must it be said?

. . .

the color, the hill, radical and going for broke
simultaneously
and echoing each other by accident
along the line of the sublimely rigid
and slanted

. . .

the only object of desire that can't be digested is memory

flouted by expression
the inaccessible

the work could be extended
the scale could be changed, requiring other decisions
improving the declaration

OVERYELLOW stretching across the hill for an entire mile
and 75 feet high
exploring an unknown limit
the immense neon speaking for my miniscule love

with a rheostat to bring on the dark or the sun

. . .

of an astonishingly docile grandeur
more powerfully affirmative than stone

dazzling and legible, appearance extends its irreversible skin
passes through us like a glance

the forest's open mouth
the explicit color, the mute poem

. . .

something else brushing up against the something
caressing the face of the same

stop running after time: settle there, make some decisions

establish the face of a second nature
of a love able to circle the earth

the color that marries as it distinguishes
the reconstructed violence

. . .

then all goes out and the mystery is revealed

ashes and flesh
finally the despair is there

a cloud of earth with all its roots

so much light it's hard to believe

while thought deftly spreads and re-emerges
knotting the night to its flash, the hill to its luxury

like the vanity of beginning
or of a painful time soon silenced

sufficient glimpse outside to divert space

the universal yellow, the confiscated royalty

to write that
captured by the culpable, which forces us to kneel

. . .

yellow is an invincible thing, concrete and internalized
like all that is governed by landscape

yellow is the interstice of all that turns out to be missing
the filter of universal fragmentation

the insistence of the place   puts all its weight on precision

lips that make
the right moment of the body touch
color on the one hand
and on the other its simple reverse, which falls

yes, the moment of the body that falls

. . .

as if yellow wandered from one reason to another
stripe by stripe

inevitable, identified

. . .

we speak with a single voice
the truest words are also arbitrary

vital yellow, scripted broom
a deluge

August 22, 2004, before the sun, everything lights up
a vanilla moment, a new planet

IV

Things bifurcate in language and there go dark.
This operation activates both their births and their ghosts. It affirms
the fact that they cannot be grasped.

Appearance provokes appearance. It gathers it, keeps it, feeds it. The
act of naming superimposes erasure; naming increases the power of
the weave of the drowning and rising. The infinitely corpuscular,
infinitely nonexistent enigma.

Becoming is a fire, though what it burns is less important than
what fans the flames and what escapes.
A sort of nervous identity rides us, passes through us. Its
insensibility needs to imprint itself on our bodies. Its matter is the
underhand of our activities, the silvering and the act of appearance.
The entire hill. Yellow and what follows.

Passing from one edge to the other while remaining on the earth, in
the same sentence, the same tearing of light.

The limit the body cannot exceed is the luck of the name, the
condition of reversal, and the passage into another thing.

Only yellow's hold, under the thousand faces of the indivisible,
only the shimmer
constant. . .

and the mute's predilection, from the counterfeiting finger
to pain's legibility,
yellow increases.

To walk with another step, exactly the same.
The unknown unforgivably betrays us.

. . .

A similar writing comes forward, beams out, and goes dark.
The broom is crossed out, the landscape biting its tongue . . .

writing shrinks

Why does it start again, and why so narrowly,
there where speech can never be accurate, and inaccurate speech
can only make a desperate attempt?

Nothing but a new murder
a spiral in the basalt
and the broom mixes the blood, turns the heart.

Soon the yellow will disperse into dissonance
soon the idiom will be beaten and the stiffness relaxed.

The falcon's pilgrimage
the target's circles

the earth turned over so its face can ring.

. . .

Sometimes, through an aristocratic terror,
writing pulverizes.
A fairy's finger points to duration.
Pierces.

By the cut, confirmed in every language, introduced in every land,
the story gets drunk.

The beautiful abstract rage
the assemblage of emotion
carried away by consequences.

. . .

A force without indulgence grows an exorbitant flower.

No word gets beyond the casing, nor the landscape's conservation.

Something swallowing imagines our fibers, ideally conveyed,
ideally phrased.

Something surpasses our arms, our craning necks, our
stretching phrases,
their failure and their mutilation.

To take the future back with each step. To stun each attempt.
Wave after wave, the hill returns, the yellow unfurls and the body
becomes unsurpassable. It terrifies itself, it buttresses itself. The
most beautiful promises of our power are its ruins, its despondency.

. . .

The landscape wanders into riotous profusion.
The hill stiffens and simplifies

the fine line aggressively thinning; the trapped aggression of
writing.

About the Author

Nicolas Pesquès (www.nicolas-pesques.fr) is the author of some fifteen volumes of poetry, the two most recent published by Flammarion. His work over the past twenty years constitutes a long meditation on the nature of language considered in relation to a mountain, Juliau, in south-central France. Two previous volumes from this series have been published in English translation—*Physis* (Parlor Press, Free Verse Editions, 2006) and *Juliology* (Counterpath, 2008). With his wife, Maïtreyi, he has co-translated a number of contemporary American poets, including Claudia Rankine and Lyn Hejinian. He has also written extensively on visual artists, including Gilles Aillaud, Aurelie Nemours, Anne Deguelle, and Paul Wallach. Active for years in animated films, he produced versions of *Tintin* and *Asterix*, among others. He lives in Paris and in the Berry.

Photograph of Nicholas Pesquès by Jean-Marc de Samie. Used by permission.

About the Translator

Cole Swensen (www.coleswensen.com) is the author of sixteen books of poetry, most recently *Landscapes on a Train* (Nightboat, 2015) and *Gravesend* (University of California, 2012). Her work has won the National Poetry Series, the Iowa Poetry Prize, and the S.F. State Poetry Center Book Award and has been short-listed for both the National Book Award and the *L.A. Times* Book Award. This is her 20th book-length translation of contemporary French experimental work. She has won the PEN USA Award in Literary Translation and has been short-listed three times for the Best Translated Book Award and once for the National Translation Award. She teaches at Brown University and divides her time between Providence, Rhode Island, and Paris, France.

Photograph of Cole Swensen by Carly Ann Faye, Pulitzer Foundation for the Arts. Used by permission.

Free Verse Editions

Edited by Jon Thompson

13 ways of happily by Emily Carr
Between the Twilight and the Sky by Jennie Neighbors
Blood Orbits by Ger Killeen
The Bodies by Chris Sindt
The Book of Isaac by Aidan Semmens
Canticle of the Night Path by Jennifer Atkinson
Child in the Road by Cindy Savett
Condominium of the Flesh by Valerio Magrelli, trans. by Clarissa Botsford
Contrapuntal by Christopher Kondrich
Country Album by James Capozzi
The Curiosities by Brittany Perham
Current by Lisa Fishman
Dismantling the Angel by Eric Pankey
Divination Machine by F. Daniel Rzicznek
Erros by Morgan Lucas Schuldt
Fifteen Seconds without Sorrow by Shim Bo-Seon, translated by Chung Eun-Gwi
    and Brother Anthony of Taizé
The Forever Notes by Ethel Rackin
The Flying House by Dawn-Michelle Baude
Go On by Ethel Rackin
Instances: Selected Poems by Jeongrye Choi, translated by Brenda Hillman,
    Wayne de Fremery, & Jeongrye Choi
The Magnetic Brackets by Jesús Losada, translated by Michael Smith &
    Luis Ingelmo
Man Praying by Donald Platt
A Map of Faring by Peter Riley
No Shape Bends the River So Long by Monica Berlin & Beth Marzoni
Overyellow by Nicolas Pesquès, translated by Cole Swensen
Physis by Nicolas Pesquès, translated by Cole Swensen
Pilgrimage Suites by Derek Gromadzki
Pilgrimly by Siobhán Scarry
Poems from above the Hill & Selected Work by Ashur Etwebi, translated by
    Brenda Hillman & Diallah Haidar
The Prison Poems by Miguel Hernández, translated by Michael Smith
Puppet Wardrobe by Daniel Tiffany
Quarry by Carolyn Guinzio
remanence by Boyer Rickel

Signs Following by Ger Killeen
Split the Crow by Sarah Sousa
Spine by Carolyn Guinzio
Spool by Matthew Cooperman
Summoned by Guillevic, translated by Monique Chefdor & Stella Harvey
Sunshine Wound by L. S. Klatt
System and Population, by Christopher Sindt
These Beautiful Limits by Thomas Lisk
They Who Saw the Deep by Geraldine Monk
The Thinking Eye by Jennifer Atkinson
This History That Just Happened by Hannah Craig
An Unchanging Blue: Selected Poems 1962–1975 by Rolf Dieter Brinkmann,
    translated by Mark Terrill
Under the Quick by Molly Bendall
Verge by Morgan Lucas Schuldt
The Wash by Adam Clay
We'll See by Georges Godeau, translated by Kathleen McGookey
What Stillness Illuminated by Yermiyahu Ahron Taub
Winter Journey [Viaggio d'inverno] by Attilio Bertolucci, translated by
    Nicholas Benson
Wonder Rooms by Allison Funk

www.ingramcontent.com/pod-product-compliance
Lightning Source LLC
Chambersburg PA
CBHW022037090426
42741CB00007B/1096